Text Structures

Lion Habitats Under Threat

A Cause and Effect Text

Phillip Simpson

Chicago, Illinois

© 2015 Heinemann Library
an imprint of Capstone Global Library, LLC
Chicago, Illinois

Edited by Diyan Leake and Kathryn Clay
Designed by Steve Mead
Picture research by Tracy Cummins
Production by Helen McCreath
Originated by Capstone Global Library Ltd

Library of Congress Cataloging-in-Publication Data
Simpson, Phillip W., 1971- author.
  Lion habitats under threat : a cause and effect text / Phillip Simpson.
       pages cm.—(Text structures)
  Summary: "This book describes how the lion population has been threatened by the destruction of its habitats. It is written primarily using the cause and effect text structure."—Provided by publisher.
  Includes bibliographical references and index.
  ISBN 978-1-4846-0417-5 (pb)
1. Lion—Juvenile literature. 2. Lion—Habitat—Conservation—Juvenile literature. 3. Habitat conservation—Juvenile literature. I. Title.

QL737.C23S56164 2015
599.757—dc23   2013040367

Photo Credits

FLPA: Elliott Neep, 17, Jean Hosking, 22; Naturepl.com: © Anup Shah, 16, 19, 20, 23, 25, © Christophe Courteau, 21, © Denis-Huot, 14, © Laurent Geslin, Front cover, © Nick Garbutt, 24, © Pete Oxford, 5, 26, © Roland Seitre, 27, © Tony Phelps, 15; Shutterstock: clickit, 11, Hedrus, 13, Jakub Krechowicz, 29 (notebook), john michael evan potter, 7, Maggy Meyer, 10, nutsiam, 12, Ohishiapply, 28, Oleg Znamenskiy, 4, spirit of america, 18, urfin, 29 (pen)

Artistic Effects

Shutterstock: kao, Olga Kovalenko, Livijus Raubickas, Peshkova, Roman Sotola

Printed in the United States of America.
092519   002751

000000LEOF14

Contents

The text in this book has been organized using the cause and effect text structure. Writers use the cause and effect text structure to explain why something has happened, and the effects it has had. To find out more about writing using this text structure, see page 28.

Some words are shown in bold, **like this**. You can find out what they mean by looking in the glossary.

What is a Lion?

The lion is a large mammal and is the second largest cat after the tiger. Lions live together in groups known as prides. They are cooperative hunters. They hunt together to catch **prey** such as gazelles and antelope. Lions are often more active at night.

Unlike other big cats, lions live in groups.

Tourists watch as lions eat their prey.

Lions used to be found in many places around the world. Thousands of years ago they were the second most widespread large land mammal after humans. Today lions are under threat because they have come into **conflict** with humans.

Lion Numbers

About 2,000 years ago scientists believed that there were more than 1 million lions on Earth. That number has steadily decreased as the human population on the planet has risen. Just 50 years ago an estimated 100,000 lions remained in Africa.

Lion population graph showing decline

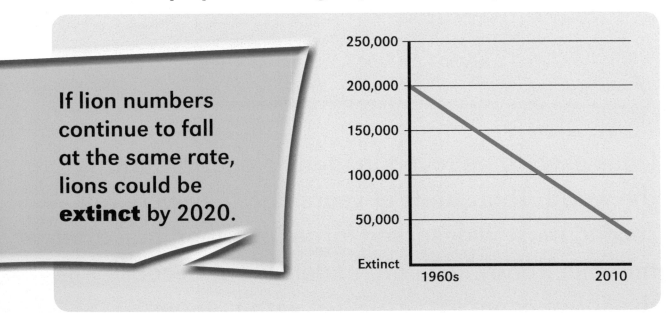

If lion numbers continue to fall at the same rate, lions could be **extinct** by 2020.

Today it is thought that there are only between 32,000 and 35,000 lions left in Africa. Of these, around 24,000 are considered to be in safe areas, where their numbers are unlikely to fall quickly. More than 6,000 lions live apart from other groups. The survival of these lions is in doubt.

Lion populations continue to drop worldwide.

Where are Lions Found?

Lions once lived in many places on Earth, such as Israel, Iraq, Pakistan, Iran, and even some parts of Europe. Today lions are mostly found in Africa. There is a small lion population in northwest India. The largest populations of lions are found in East Africa and Southern Africa.

Map showing the different areas of Africa

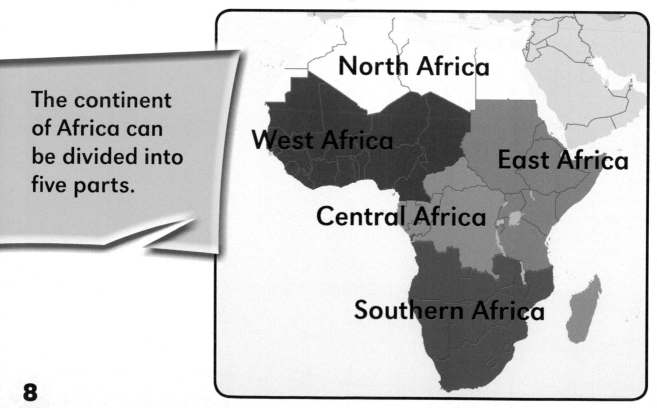

The continent of Africa can be divided into five parts.

North Africa

West Africa

East Africa

Central Africa

Southern Africa

In countries such as Benin in West Africa there are only about 480 lions. In Central Africa there are about 2,500 lions. There are almost 20,000 lions still living in East Africa, with the greatest numbers in Tanzania. About 12,000 lions live in Southern Africa.

Map showing where lions live in Africa

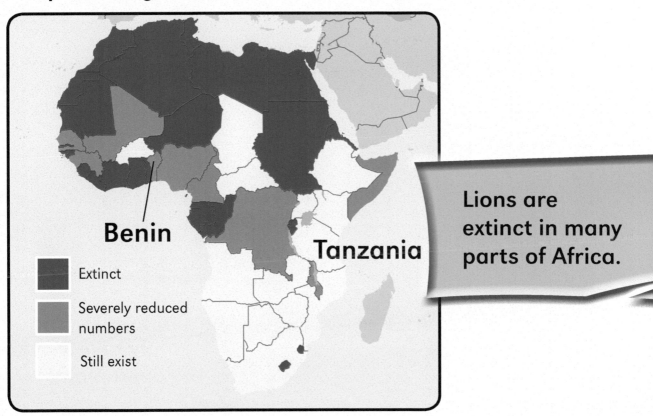

Benin

Tanzania

Extinct

Severely reduced numbers

Still exist

Lions are extinct in many parts of Africa.

What is a habitat?

A **habitat** is the type of environment in which a plant or animal lives. The climate, or weather in a place, and the geography of habitats are usually different from one another. A habitat might have rain forests, grasslands, deserts, and plains.

Lions are most commonly found on the open plains of Africa.

A habitat needs to have everything an animal or plant needs to live, including food and water. Lions are **carnivores**, or meat eaters. Their food includes prey animals such as antelope.

An animal needs food, water, and shelter to survive in a habitat.

Lion Habitats

A lion's habitat is usually grassland such as a **savannah**. In this type of habitat there are many open plains filled with shrubs and grasses that can survive with little or no rain. Acacia and baobab trees are spaced out across the plains.

Trees are dotted across savannahs.

In the wet season there is plenty of prey for lions.

Rather than seasons like summer and winter in a savannah, there are periods of wet and dry weather. During the wet season the grasses and shrubs grow. These plants provide food and water for grazing animals, such as antelope and zebras. Lions hunt many of these animals.

Causes of Lion Habitat Destruction

Lion habitats are under threat because of humans. Many savannah areas where lions live are being taken over by humans. These areas are used for farmland and to make room for rising human populations.

For many people, farming is their only source of income.

Savannahs and woodlands are being destroyed to build houses for humans.

For a long time global maps have shown savannahs and woodlands covering large areas of Africa. Scientists have used **satellite imagery** to show that this is no longer the case. Many of these areas are now filled with fields and houses, destroying the lion's habitat.

Humans and Lions

Lions need a large habitat to survive. They are forced to move often, following the herds of animals that they hunt. Because of the dry seasons, lions must keep moving around their **territory** in order to find water. As a result they sometimes come into contact with humans. This can lead to conflict.

Lions must keep moving to find food and water.

Sometimes lions are forced to feed on cattle.

Lions that enter areas where people live cannot find their normal food. As a result they find animals that humans need to survive, such as cattle. Lions often attack these animals because they are easy prey. Occasionally, even humans are attacked by lions.

Effects of Lion Habitat Destruction

As human numbers continue to rise, they need more space in which to live. This results in the constant destruction of the lion's habitat, which has a huge impact on the entire **ecosystem**. Plants and animals form part of an ecosystem, which also includes air, water, and soil.

Large farmlands continue to destroy lion habitats.

As lion numbers fall, other **predators** such as hyenas take their place.

Plants and animals within an ecosystem depend on each other to survive. If lion numbers continue to fall, other smaller carnivores will take their place. This will have an impact on other plants and animals.

What Can Be Done?

It is possible to **preserve** lion numbers and even increase them. One of the biggest problems is when humans and lions come in contact with each other. **Livestock** fences are being strengthened to stop lion attacks. If the lions are unable to kill livestock, then humans are unlikely to hunt and kill the lions.

Building stronger fences will keep lions from attacking livestock.

Teaching people about the importance of animals will help conservation efforts.

One of the main ways to help lions is to learn more about them. Humans are slowly starting to understand how important lions are because of their position in the ecosystem. Local people are starting to realize that killing lions is not a good way to protect their livestock.

Game Reserves

Game reserves are areas set aside for wildlife. They are very important for saving lions. In these areas lions are safe from being hunted. Few humans are allowed to use the land for farming or building houses.

People working on game reserves help keep lions protected.

The human population continues to rise. Therefore, we need to grow more food and provide more houses. However, since the land on game reserves can rarely be used for this purpose, it stops the lion's habitat from being destroyed. As a result humans and lions are less likely to come into conflict with each other.

Lions are much safer within game reserves.

Serengeti National Park, Tanzania

Serengeti National Park in Tanzania has almost 3.7 million acres of savannah, which is the perfect habitat for lions. The park has millions of prey animals, such as wildebeests and gazelles.

The Serengeti National Park is one of the most important game reserves for all animals, including lions.

The park is home to about 4,000 lions. The lions are free to move around in their natural habitat and are unlikely to come into conflict with humans. Only the local tribe of Maasai is allowed to live in this area, and their numbers and farms are small.

Lions thrive in the Serengeti National Park.

Tourism

The lion is one of the most recognizable and loved animals in the world. As a result, people come from all over the world to see the lion in its natural habitat. People in Africa are beginning to understand that the destruction of the lion's habitat means that tourists will no longer be able to see the lion in the wild.

On safari, tourists can see lions in their natural habitat.

Game reserves provide lion habitats and create jobs for local people.

Tourism brings a lot of money into Africa. Many people go on safaris, where they pay to see animals. More money can be made by preserving the lion's habitat than by using the land for farming or housing.

Explanation of Text Structure

This text focuses on **cause and effect**. A cause is the reason something has happened. The effect is what has happened as a result of it. In this type of text, words such as *because*, *since,* and *as a result* help to explain what causes something to happen.

The human population continues to rise. Therefore, we need to grow more food and provide more houses. However, since the land on game reserves can rarely be used for this purpose, it stops the lion's habitat from being destroyed. As a result humans and lions are less likely to come into conflict with each other.

Cause and effect words

Now you could try using the **cause and effect** text structure to write about:

- tsunamis
- cloud formation
- thunder and lightning

Glossary

carnivore an animal that eats meat

conflict a struggle

ecosystem plants and animals that are found in a particular area and depend on each other for survival

extinct no longer existing

habitat a natural home for an animal or plant

livestock farm animals

predator an animal that hunts and eats other animals

preserve to keep safe

prey an animal that is hunted and eaten by other animals

satellite imagery pictures sent back from equipment far above Earth

savannah a large area of grassland

territory an area that an animal thinks of as its own

Find Out More

Books

Bodden, Valerie. *Lions.* Animals are Amazing. Mankato, Minn.: Creative Education, 2010.

Guillain, Charlotte. *Mighty Lions.* Walk on the Wild Side. Chicago: Raintree, 2013.

Websites

www.bbc.co.uk/nature/life/Lion
This site has some amazing videos of lions.

gowild.wwf.org.uk/africa
Visit the World Wildlife Fund's Go Wild section to learn more about lions and where they live.

www.kids.nationalgeographic.com/kids/animals/creaturefeature/lion
National Geographic's website includes lots of interesting lion facts.

www.sciencekids.co.nz/sciencefacts/animals/lion.html
Find out more about lions on this website.

Index